COUNTING MONEY

by Tanya Thayer

first step nonfiction

Lerner Publications Company · Minneapolis

I can **count money.**

I can count **cents.**

I have a **penny.**

It is 1 cent.

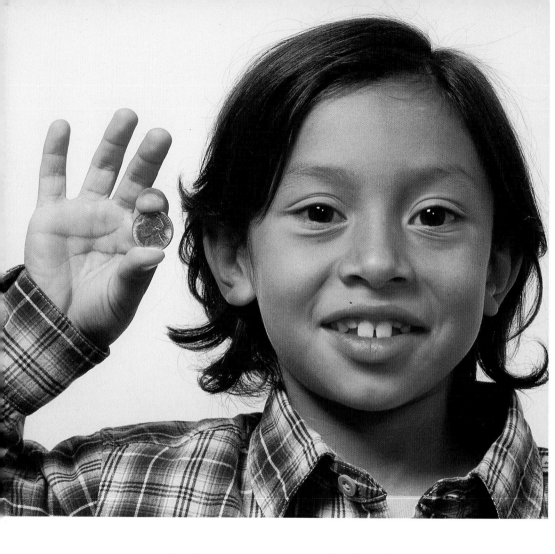

I have a nickel.

It is 5 cents.

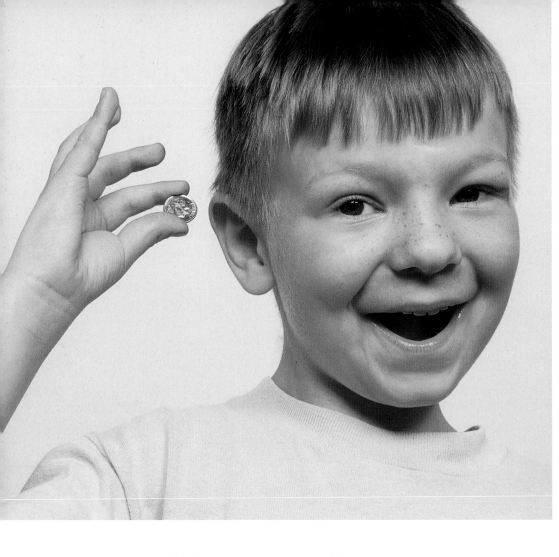

I have a dime.

It is 10 cents.

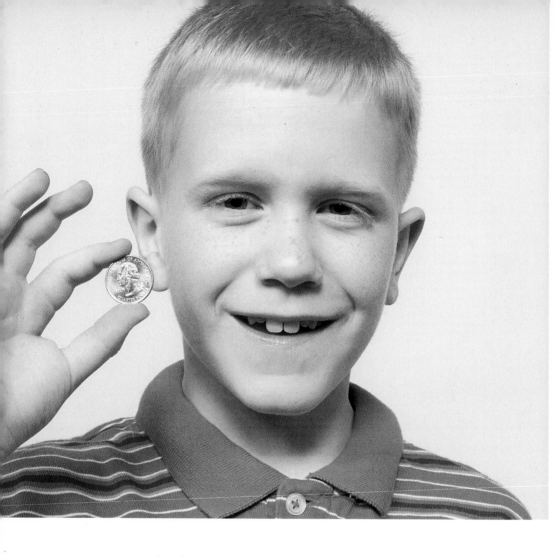

I have a **quarter.**

 = 25¢

It is 25 cents.

I have a dollar.

It is 100 cents.

I have 1 penny, 1 nickel, 1 dime, 1 quarter, and 1 dollar.

I have 1 dollar and
41 cents.

I can count money.

Counting money is fun.

5 pennies equal 1 nickel

2 nickels equal 1 dime

10 dimes equal 1 dollar

5 nickels equal 1 quarter

2 quarters equal a half dollar

=50¢

4 quarters equal 1 dollar

=$1.00

Counting Money Facts

 If you have three quarters, four dimes, and four pennies, you have $1.19. You also have the largest amount of money in coins without being able to make change for a dollar.

 The dollar bill has many 13's. The eagle on the back is holding 13 arrows and an olive branch with 13 leaves. Above it is a badge with 13 stars.

There are 293 ways to make change for a dollar!

 Currency is paper money, or folding money.

 Dollars are made of paper that is made out of cotton.

 Pennies are made of copper.

 Paper money was first used in China.

Glossary

 cent – an amount of money

 count – to add something together

 money – what people use to buy things

 penny – a coin that equals 1 cent

 quarter – a coin that equals 25 cents

Index

The photographs in this book are reproduced through the courtesy of: Corbis Royalty Free, front cover; Todd Strand/IPS, 2, 4, 5, 6, 7, 8, 9, 10, 11, 13, 15, 22 (top, 2nd from top, 2nd from bottom, bottom); © Laura Dwight/CORBIS, 3; © Julie Toy/Stone, 12; © N. Alexander/Visuals Unlimited, 14; © EyeWire Royalty Free, 16; © Diane Meyer, 17, 22 (middle).

Lerner Publications Company
A division of Lerner Publishing Group
241 First Avenue North
Minneapolis, MN 55401 U.S.A.

Website address: www.lernerbooks.com

Library of Congress Cataloging-in-Publication Data

Thayer, Tanya.
    Counting money / by Tanya Thayer.
        p.   cm. — (First step nonfiction)
    Includes index.
    Summary: Presents an overview of the number of cents in a penny, a nickel, a dime, a quarter, and a dollar.
        ISBN 0-8225-1258-0
        1. Counting—Juvenile literature. 2. Money—Juvenile literature. [1. Money. 2. Counting.]
    I. Title. II. Series.
    QA113 .T46 2002
    513.2'11—dc21   2001002449

Manufactured in the United States of America
2 3 4 5 6 7 – DP – 10 09 08 07 06 05